Animals

Edward Hicks. (1780 - 1849)
The Peaceable Kingdom
Collection of Edgar William and Bernice Chrysler Garbisch

GOD'S
Faithful Servants

Dr. Joe King

❀ ❀ ❀ *Animals* ❀ ❀ ❀

© 1997 SunDance Press - Dr. Joe King

All rights reserved

Library of Congress in Publication Data

1. Animals - religious outlook
2. Animals - scientific views
3. Animals - spirit

ISBN 0-944551-24-6

FIRST EDITION

1 2 3 4 5 6 7 8 9 10

Printed in El Paso, Texas, USA
on recycled acid free paper
with soybean - based ink

Design by Michael R. Moses
Editing by Grant Caldwell
Paintings from the traditional era

Typefaces used are
Optimum Roman &
Rose Round

Sun
Dance
Press

Dr. Joe King

Contents
(All Biblical refererences from the New American Standard Version)

Introduction

1. Man and Animal

2. Science and Faith

3. Do Animals go to Heaven

4. Dealing with Grief

5. Euthanasia

6. Funeral Services for Pets

Appendices

A. Prayers and Blessings for Animals

B. Bible References to Animals

❧ ❧ ❧ *Animals* ❧ ❧ ❧

Dedicated
to all the animals that have graced my life
and to the Creator of us all.

Edward Hicks. (1780 - 1849)
Noah's Ark

❧ ❧ ❧   Dr. Joe King   ❧ ❧ ❧

Introduction

From a very early age, two basic desires dominated my thoughts. One, I wanted to be a veterinarian. Two, I felt a strong need to serve God. Even though it never happened, I spent most of my life preparing to go to some third world country as a veterinary missionary. I fulfilled much of that desire by pastoring churches on the US/Mexico border and by spending much of my ministry working with agriculturists, animal scientists, doctors, nurses and veterinarians providing humanitarian services to remote areas along the border and deep into the interior of Mexico.

In college and seminary I was taught that the difference between man and animals is that man has a soul, animals do not. As a minister, I taught faithfully what I had been taught. Often, I was asked questions dealing with animal theology. Having never studied specifically

❖ ❖ ❖ *Animals* ❖ ❖ ❖

about animal theology, I would try to piece together an answer based on what I had been taught and what I had read. What really amazed me was that there were no books on the subject. It was during this time that I began a journey through the Bible and historical literature that would last for almost ten years. The conclusions of my studies and observations have surfaced as a series of books, this being the first.

Animals have and will throughout eternity be a part of God's plan. God created animals to be companions for man. Animals have suffered the consequences of man's fall from grace and when God restores man from that fall, the animals will benefit.

To the theological community, this book may be controversial. Like many, for years I taught what I had been taught. Through intense study, diligent prayer and much travail, I am convinced that I was taught wrong when it comes to animals. Animals are spiritual creatures and man constantly needs to be reminded of that.

❖ ❖ ❖ Dr. Joe King ❖ ❖ ❖

To the animal lovers of this world this book offers no surprise, just confirmation. To those who have lost a pet, are considering euthanasia, or to those looking for some solace as to what part our pets play throughout eternity, I pray that this book brings peace and comfort.

❖ ❖ ❖ *Animals* ❖ ❖ ❖

Giotto (1267 - 1337)
The flight into Egypt (c.1304 - 06)
Fresco, Arena (*Scrovegni*) Chapel, Padua

"Then God said, 'Let Us make man in Our image, according to Our likeness; and let them rule over the fish of the sea and over the birds of the sky and over the cattle and over all the earth, and over every creeping thing that creeps on the earth."

(Genesis 1:26)

Man and Animal

Veterinarians have a very unique task in that they must be able to treat a wide range of species ranging from moles to monkeys. Each species has unique characteristics that separates it from the others.

There are anatomical differences. This can be illustrated by the fact that man has a gall bladder but horses do not. There are the differences in digestive tracts seen in ruminants (i.e. cows and goats) and monogastric animals (i.e. dogs, horses and man). Horses have one small stomach and cattle have four. In the study of veterinary medicine, students learn comparative anatomy. In my case, I studied the anatomy of the horse and then compared every other species to the horse. You can appreciate the wide range of differences when you look at the anatomy of a horse and then compare it to that of a chicken. In human medicine the major distinctions are among men, women and children.

There are the physiological differences among species. These include differences in temperature, heart rate, respiration, gestation period, life span or the number of young born to any given species. Physiological distinctions between species such as blood counts, blood chemistry, length of estrus and urine production are all critical to understanding each species.

All of these differences require each species to be treated different in diet, nutrition, examination, restraint, and, eventually, medically, when treated.

There are differences in intelligence. Man's intelligence is a measurement of intelligence quotient (IQ). IQ is based on how well one scores on an intelligence test compared to how well others scored on the same exam. Animal intelligence is determined by how well a particular animal solves a difficult problem. If we were to list animals according to their level of intelligence the list would look something this:

❖ ❖ ❖ Dr. Joe King ❖ ❖ ❖

Monkeys and Apes

Ocean Mammals
(dolphins and whales)

Flesh eating mammals
(dogs and cats)

Hoofed animals
(horses and cows)

Rodents

Birds

Amphibians and Reptiles

Fish

Animals without backbones

When the Bible states *"... and God made the beast of the earth after their kind, and the cattle after their kind, and every thing that creepeth upon the earth after its kind..." (Genesis 1:25)*, it is easy to understand how each species is unique to itself even though there are similarities that bind us all together.

There is another major distinction that must be

🐾 🐾 🐾 *Animals* 🐾 🐾 🐾

made between man and animals. *"Then God said, 'Let Us make man in Our own image, according to Our likeness; and let them rule over the fish of the sea and over the birds of the sky and over the cattle and over all the earth, and over every creeping thing that creeps on the earth'" (Genesis 1:26).* Man was made in the image of God and animals were not.

The full significance of this passage has been debated by theologians and academia for centuries. The significance of being made "in the image of God," is still being debated today. Explanations have ranged from being similar in appearance, in spiritual nature, to knowing the difference between good and evil. God creates, man is creative! Man makes choices, animals do not! Man, through his intellectual prowess can design, manufacture, change his surroundings, change his environment and his fate. Through his freedom of choice man can choose to worship and serve his creator. This freedom also gives him the ability not to choose.

When we look at the animal kingdom, we can

🐾 🐾 🐾 Dr. Joe King 🐾 🐾 🐾

be certain animals have very little choice. Animals can be made to serve man and are often the victims of man's choices. Man can choose to serve God but animals cannot choose to serve man. The reality is, animals must live with man's choices whether it is to their benefit or their demise.

Not only was man made in the image of God, but the Bible states that man was given dominion over the animals. It is easy to understand why this is so: Man through his superior intellect, ability to create and his freedom of choice can use all of his ability to dominate those animals around him. This freedom of choice enables man to wipe-out extinct species, make decisions of life and death, and abuse or mistreat the animals that are dependent upon him for survival.

"Made in the image of God" carries enormous responsibility!

❖ ❖ ❖ *Animals* ❖ ❖ ❖

Master of the St. Francis Cycle.
St Francis Preaching to the Birds. (c.1297 - 1300)
Fresco, Upper church of San Francesco, Assisi

Science And Faith

Science is the product of known facts, the observable conclusions of repeated experiments. In science, all observations are governed by principles. Scientists draw conclusions through a process known as "The Scientific Method." This method begins with a stated problem, the scientist then forms an hypothesis, observes and experiments, interprets the information gathered during experimentation and ultimately draws a conclusion. In science, something is true when it can be repeated.

Faith is the complete antithesis of science. Faith is the ability to accept something as true or proven even though it can't be observed. Faith is the ability to walk forward without being able to see the road beneath your feet. Faith is accepting certain principles as truth even though those principles cannot be touched, tested or proven.

The best definition of faith is found in He-

❖ ❖ ❖ *Animals* ❖ ❖ ❖

brew 11:1. *"Now faith is the assurance of things hoped for, the conviction of things not seen."*

When science and faith are merged, we must remember; one is proven and tested through repeated observations and the other is the ability to accept something without proof or testing. How does one prove the existence of God? The existence of God is accepted by faith and not through scientific observations. The same is true for the soul of man or animal. Does man have a soul? How do you know? It is through faith we conclude that man is a spiritual being and has a soul. It is through faith that man will accept the fact that animals are spiritual beings. I do believe that, in time, scientists will be able to prove the existence of soul and spirit. Near death experiences, life after life and other issues of a spiritual nature have been the subject of many books and discussions in recent years.

For me, the merging of science and faith was not so difficult. Let me explain. As a child, from grade school through college, I was taught scientific theory. In high school and college I studied mathematics, biol-

❖ ❖ ❖ Dr. Joe King ❖ ❖ ❖

ogy, physics, and chemistry. I was taught how to conduct scientific experiments, make observations and eventually draw conclusions. Simple scientific observations like identifying the boiling point of water were repeated over and over throughout the years until the principles of the scientific method became second nature.

Principles of faith were a constant part of my childhood. I grew up in church, was part of a very spiritual family, attended a church university, and studied at a theological seminary. At the same time I was being taught scientific theory in grade school I was being taught principles of faith in church. While studying theology in college I took courses in physics, biology and chemistry. There was never a time I felt a conflict in principle.

In the world of science we have no problem accepting certain truths without being able to explain the scientific theory behind them; fire burns, water flows downhill, water boils when heated, airplanes fly and the earth orbits the sun. There are certain prin-

❖ ❖ ❖ *Animals* ❖ ❖ ❖

ciples that regulate our universe. There are principles that govern every single thing we do and we accept them without being able to explain the details of their existence.

In the world of faith there are certain principles that govern our everyday lives. Like scientific law, there are spiritual laws or truths that define every aspect of our lives. These laws or principles were set in motion at the creation of the universe and are absolute truth. Everything in the universe exists and behaves according to these truths. In the scientific community we define these truths as law and in the spiritual community we define them as principles of faith, prayer being a prime example. Recent studies have shown that patients in hospitals who are prayed for leave sooner, heal faster and have fewer complications. How does prayer work? I don't know, but it works!

If you can imagine, at the creation of the universe, principles were established that govern everything in the universe. This includes spiritual laws as well as physical laws. Man is only beginning to under-

Dr. Joe King

stand the physical world. Look at what has happened during the last 100 years; the airplane, automobile, space travel, electronic communications and the computer. What will we discover in the next 100 years? What will we learn about the spiritual and physical nature of man?

In medical school I studied physiology. Physiology taught me that the normal body behaves in a given and predictable manner. Healthy cells have a predictable appearance and behave in a predictable way. Pathology taught me that the body behaves differently when under attack or when diseased or traumatized. Physiology and pathology are taught disciplines. I went to class and was taught principles that I accepted as fact. In the beginning I trusted the professors to be knowledgeable and factual. Through trial and error I learned that what was taught was trustworthy and reliable. Today, some of the things I was taught as being absolute are being challenged and may very well be wrong. This does not mean that those classes were of no value, classes were taught using the best body of information available

Animals

at the time.

After five years of medical classes, I found that I could predict with some accuracy how the healthy body should respond and how disease and trauma could alter that response. Again, the diseased body produces predictable results. When one recognizes particular clinical signs as common to a known disease, he can then treat that disease and expect other predictable results. Thus, through the process of study, education and observations, the uneducated becomes educated and what was unknown becomes known.

Learning to accept matters of faith as matters of fact is a learning process. Through trial and error, the school of hard knocks, I learned to appropriate faith into my daily life. We must all become seekers of information. We must test what we don't know against what we know. We must put what we have been taught to the test of daily observation.

Only then can faith and science find a com-

Dr. Joe King

fortable place in our lives. Accepting something as fact only because someone has declared it as fact is a dangerous position.

I was taught in seminary and college that the difference between man and animal was that man had a soul and animals did not. For years, I taught what I had been taught. Deep inside there was an agonizing conflict between what I was teaching and what I believed to be true. After sixteen years of ministry, years of theological training and five years of medical school, I can say without a doubt that indeed animals have souls. Animals are spiritual creatures, made by God and a part of His eternal plan.

Please don't put the cart before the horse! Prior to accepting this as a matter of fact in your own life, deal with your own doubts. You must first deal with the soul of man. Is man an eternal being, made by God, spiritual in design? If you are struggling with your own spirituality, you will find it very difficult to deal with the spirituality of the animals.

Animals

Bartolomé Esteban Murillo (1618 - 1682)
The Annunciation. c.1660 -1664
Prado, Madrid

Do Animals go to Heaven?

Man was created to serve God and animals were created to serve man. It is through the diligent service to man that animals become God's Faithful Servants. Animals provide companionship to man, food, clothing, shelter, medicine, research and services beyond mention. Animals daily give their lives in the service to man. Animals serve God well! If man could only be so faithful! Since the beginning of recorded history, animals have played an integral part in God's eternal plan. Parents can tell their children with confidence that the pets that have served them so well do have a special place in God's kingdom; in the past, present and the future.

Let's look at the Biblical references to animals in service to God and man and also to the numerous references to animals throughout eternity. In the beginning, animals were created to be companions to man. Like man, the animals were formed from the dust of the ground.

❧ ❧ ❧ *Animals* ❧ ❧ ❧

God formed every living creature and took them to man to be named:

> *"Then the Lord God said, 'It is not good for the man to be alone; I will make him a helper suitable for him.' And out of the ground the Lord God formed every beast of the field and every bird of the sky, and brought them to the man to see what he would call them; and whatever the man called a creature, that was its name. And the man gave names to all the cattle, and to the birds of the sky, and to every beast of the field,..." (Genesis 2:18-20)*

In early Genesis God destroyed the world by flood but spared Noah, his family, and representatives of all living species by commanding Noah to build an ark. Clean animals, those acceptable for sacrifice, were taken into the ark by sevens. Unclean animals, those not acceptable form sacrifice, were taken into the ark by twos (Genesis 7:8-9).

It was not until after the Genesis flood that man

🐾 🐾 🐾 Dr. Joe King 🐾 🐾 🐾

and animals became carnivores. Until this time in history, man and animals had been vegetarians (Genesis 9:2-3). It is after the Genesis flood that God placed the fear of man upon the animal kingdom and man and animals became meat eaters.

After the Genesis flood, God established a covenant with Noah and the animal kingdom agreeing never again to destroy the world by flood. Most people never realize that this covenant was an agreement between God, man, and all living creatures. The rainbow was given to man and the animal kingdom as a sign of this agreement.

"And God said, 'This is the sign of the covenant which I am making between Me and you and every living creature that is with you, for all successive generations.'" (Genesis 9:12)

A covenant is an agreement. In order to seal that agreement, God placed a rainbow in the sky as a physical reminder of the agreement between Himself, man, and the animal kingdom.

❖ ❖ ❖ *Animals* ❖ ❖ ❖

Throughout the bible there are stories of God using animals to teach spiritual truths and preserve mankind. God uses a donkey to teach Balaam to listen to God and to open his eyes to the spiritual things around him. Balaam's donkey sees the angel of the Lord when Balaam and his servants cannot. God also gives the donkey the ability to speak and by so doing, opens the eyes of Balaam to the spiritual things around him and to the will of God (Numbers 22:21-35). Is it possible that God uses the animals around us to reveal basic spiritual truths? More than likely it happens more often than we realize.

God used ravens to feed the prophet Elijah in the wilderness. God told Elijah that He had commanded the ravens to provide for him while hiding by a brook. The ravens brought Elijah bread and meat in the morning and bread and meat in the evening (I Kings 17:4,6).

In the book of Jonah, God appointed a great fish to protect Jonah from the raging sea by swallowing him. After three days and nights in the belly of the fish, God commanded the fish to spit Jonah onto dry ground, safe

Dr. Joe King

and secure (Jonah 2:10). After his encounter with the fish, Jonah was more willing to listen to the voice of God (Jonah 3:1-3).

If you think of all the animal encounters you have experienced, it is very easy to conceive how God could bring an animal into your life to teach you very simple spiritual lessons. One unique attribute of a pet is unconditional love. Pets love us in spite of our failures, blemishes or shortcomings. Is that not much like the love of God, unconditional?

Not only did God create the animal kingdom, He declared that they belong to him. The Psalmist wrote: *"Every beast of the forest is Mine, The cattle on a thousand hills. I know every bird of the mountain, And everything that moves in the field is mine..."* (Psalms 50:10-11).

The writer of Psalms 104 describes the Lord as the creator of the heavens and earth. In this passage the writer describes how God prepared the earth for all living creatures and declares: *"...Thou dost take away their spirit,*

❖ ❖ ❖ *Animals* ❖ ❖ ❖

they expire, And return to their dust. Thou dost send forth Thy Spirit, they are created..." (Psalms 104:29,30)

Theologically speaking, Psalms 104 is a parallel passage to Genesis chapter 1. The writer of this passage believed that the animal kingdom was created by God and the life- giving force enabling animals to exist and live was through the presence of God's Spirit (Psalms 104:29-30). In Elihu's speech to Job, Elihu declares: *"The Spirit of God has made me, And the breath of the Almighty gives me life" (Job 33:4).*

Elihu goes on to declare to Joab: *"If He should determine to do so, If He should gather to Himself His spirit and His breath, All flesh would perish together" (Job 34:14,15).*

Even though Elihu has a somewhat distorted view of Job's problems, his statement is a reflection of the common thought of his day; It is the Spirit of God that gives life to man and animals (All flesh).

❖ ❖ ❖ Dr. Joe King ❖ ❖ ❖

Isaiah, the Old Testament prophet, spoke of a time when God would restore the earth to a place of peaceful coexistence. It is during this period of time that God will remove the impact that the "fall of man" had upon the animal kingdom. Isaiah declares: *"...the wolf will dwell with the Lamb...the leopard will lie down with the kid...the calf and the young lion and the fatling together ...and a little boy will lead them...the cow and the bear will graze ...their young will lie down together; and the lion will eat straw like the ox...and the nursing child will play by the hole of the cobra...and the weaned child will put his hand on the viper's den. They will not hurt or destroy in all My holy mountain...." (Isaiah 11:6-9).*

Isaiah describes a time when the earth is no longer impacted by ramifications of man's fall from grace. It is interesting to note that man and animals were vegetarians until after the Genesis flood and in this passage, once again, "... *the lion will eat straw like the ox.*"

In the New Testament there are many references to animals serving the Son of God and man. Jesus was

❖ ❖ ❖ *Animals* ❖ ❖ ❖

born in a stable surrounded by animals (Luke 2:7). The Holy Spirit comes to Jesus as a dove after His baptism (Mark 1:10). After Jesus was baptized, He was tempted by Satan, during this time Jesus *"...was with the wild beast, and the angels were ministering to Him" (Mark 1:13).* Jesus told his disciples that sparrows were sold in the market place for one cent but not one falls to the ground without His knowledge (Matthew 10:29). Luke, the beloved physician and gospel writer said that not one of them (sparrow) is forgotten by God (Luke 12:6). Not only is God omniscient, knowing everything, His awareness of the death of a sparrow should be very comforting to us, especially regarding our pets.

In Mark, Jesus gives permission to an unclean spirit to enter a herd of swine (Mark 5:13f). He feeds the multitudes by multiplying the loaves of bread and fish (Mark 6:30f).

Jesus enters Jerusalem on the back of a young donkey colt. In this case, a young donkey, never before ridden. There is much more to this story than meets the

❖ ❖ ❖ Dr. Joe King ❖ ❖ ❖

eye. A young colt, unbroken, carries the Master through the streets of Jerusalem with crowds waving palm branches and their robes while they cheer. This young colt donkey understood his mission and served the Master well. Throughout the New Testament you see animals as God's Faithful Servants.

The book of Revelation is written to the Church during a time when Christians were being threatened by Rome. The book is apocalyptic in nature, rich in symbolism, and rich in animal references. There are the four living creatures surrounding the throne of God. One is like a lion, the second like a calf, the third has a face like a man and the fourth is like a flying eagle. Each one has six wings, is full of eyes and, day and night, gives glory and honor and thanks to God (Revelation 4:4-8). Ezekiel describes a similar vision in his book (Ezekiel 1:4-14). Some say that these creatures are angels or cherubim. Whatever they are, they are like man and the animals God created and they continually praise God. It is my opinion that these living creatures represent all of God's creation. These verses describe things to come . The author de-

❖ ❖ ❖ *Animals* ❖ ❖ ❖

scribes a scene in which "…every created thing which is in heaven and on the earth, and under the earth and on the sea, and all things in them…" praise "Him who sits on the throne, and to the Lamb…"(Revelation 5:13).

Throughout the book animals are strongly used to describe the things to come in Revelation. A white, red, black and ashen horse brings the sealed judgments of God (Revelation 6:2,4,5, and 8). An eagle flying in mid-heaven announces the coming judgment (Revelation 8:13) also prior to the battle of Armageddon (Revelation 19:17).

Do animals go to heaven? One thing is for sure, There is never a time in the Holy Scriptures when you fail to see representatives of the animal kingdom. When God destroyed the world by flood, He spared Noah, his family and representatives of all living creatures. When God restores the earth to a time of perfect peace, the lion is there with the lamb. When He returns to collect the saints for eternity, the animals are there.

Yes, animals go to heaven.

❀ ❀ ❀ Dr. Joe King ❀ ❀ ❀

Raphael
The Miraculous Draught of Fishes (1515)
The Victoria and Albert Museum, London

Animals

Master of Seo de Urgel
St. Jerome the Penitent (c.1597-1600)
Museum of Catalan Art, Barcelona

Dealing with the Loss of a Pet

The loss of a pet can be as dramatic and devastating as the loss of a spouse, parent, child or a very close friend. As a pastor I have seen lives shattered by the death of a spouse, son or daughter. As a veterinarian, I have seen men and women break down and enter periods of deep depression when a companion pet dies.

Death is a fact of life! Not only must we deal with the death of those who are close to us, we will probably have to deal with the death of several pets during our lifetime and, eventually, our own mortality.

Counselors tell us that when faced with a significant loss in our life, humans go through a series of steps in dealing with that loss. In most people the grieving process includes several stages of grief:

1. Denial

❖ ❖ ❖ *Animals* ❖ ❖ ❖

2. Anger

3. Bargaining

4. Depression

5. Acceptance

6. Hope

Denial is the refusal to accept the reality of a sickness, death or loss. Many times the owner of a pet will refuse to acknowledge the news of a pet's terminal illness or eventual death. Many will seek a second or third opinion, hoping to receive information contrary to the original diagnosis or opinion. When told of the death of a pet many will initially refuse to accept that news.

Anger is the stage where one tries to blame something or someone for the loss. Many will hide their anger, blame God, blame the veterinarian or even themselves. Also many times guilt will be associated with anger. Anger is part of the process and can last for long periods of time if allowed to. Friends trying to help a grieving friend should realize that anger is part of the pro-

Dr. Joe King

cess but it will pass.

Bargaining is the process where we try to make a deal with God. Some try to promise God a lifetime of service and commitment if He only will restore their loss. I think that many feel that bargaining is a last ditch effort to change the inevitable. This may be the last remnant of hope that exists prior to accepting the reality of our loss.

Depression comes after one realizes that the loss is real, anger has subsided and one then realizes that no bargains can be struck. For the first time one begins to acknowledge the certainty of their loss. Their loss is real! Hopelessness prevails and one realizes their loss cannot be challenged.

Acceptance is the final step prior to recovery when associated with a death. Acceptance means that one cannot change the outcome, the death is factual, there was no mistake.

Eventually, given a chance, hope will prevail. You

Animals

must go on! Life continues and in spite of your loss, you must continue forward.

While serving as a student chaplain in college, I was placed in a rotation on the terminal patient ward of a hospital in Dallas. During that time I was taught, and it was confirmed over and over again to me, that the grieving process is true of those who lose loved ones, are told of terminal diseases, and in many cases common to those undergoing divorce, the loss of a job or who face other significant losses in life.

As a veterinarian, I realized that those same reactions to death or loss mentioned above were also the reactions I observed in pet owners when faced with the loss of a beloved pet. The human mind grieves the loss of a pet the same way it grieves the loss of loved family member. Different people deal with grief in different ways. Not everyone displays the typical signs of grief and not everyone goes through the process in the typical order. Grief can be short-term and, in some people's lives, it seems to last for eternity.

🐾 🐾 🐾 Dr. Joe King 🐾 🐾 🐾

To veterinarians reading this book I say, do not belittle the impact that the loss of a pet has on the human spirit.

To pet owners I say, do not despair, have hope, death is not the end but to us all, a beginning. There is hope for the bereaved! Here are some things you can do to help cope with your loss.

1. Understand that grieving is part of the healing process and the loss of a pet can be significant.

2. Surround yourself with people who understand your loss.

3. If possible and available, join a support group.

4. Try not to make major decisions while grieving. It is best to postpone life changing decisions.

5. Seek professional help. There are compassionate veterinarians ministers, and even professional counselors who will help you to deal with your loss.

6. It is very important that you take care of yourself. Eat right, exercise and do not neglect your own well-being.

7. Remember, time does heal.

8. Ask God to give you strength and understanding.

❦ ❦ ❦ *Animals* ❦ ❦ ❦

To those who have a friend that has suffered a significant loss, here are some things you can do to help speed their recovery.

1. You should understand the grieving process.

2. At the beginning you need to say very little, just listen and be a friend.

3. Give your friend a copy of this book or another book on grief.

4. Do not belittle the loss of a pet.

5. If appropriate, help your friend find a professional counselor.

6. If appropriate, help your friend plan a memorial service.

7. Pray for your friend.

❖ ❖ ❖ Dr. Joe King ❖ ❖ ❖

Botticelli (1444/45 - 1510)
The Nativity (Detail)
National Gallery, London

❖ ❖ ❖ *Animals* ❖ ❖ ❖

Albrecht Durer (1471 1528)
Praying Hands
Graphische Sammlung Albertina, Vienna

Euthanasia

Euthanasia has been the most difficult aspect of veterinary medicine I have had to deal with. Prior to putting an animal to sleep I thank God for the life of the animal, for his or her faithfulness to God and Man and ask God to bless this animal in death. It is a tough area.

Let's begin with the question, "Do we have a right to end the life of an animal?" All of our decisions in life are based on principles we have been taught or learned during our lifetime. These principles we have been taught or learned are then validated by our own consciences. This book addresses issues from a Judeo-Christian theological perspective, and my belief system has been derived from those principles. God created animals as companions for man (Genesis 2:18-20). After the fall of man (Genesis 3) and the Genesis Flood (Genesis 6-8), God placed the fear of man upon all the animal kingdom and gave man dominion over it and also the right to use "…every moving thing that is alive as food. (Genesis 9:1-3).

❖ ❖ ❖ *Animals* ❖ ❖ ❖

After the Genesis flood Noah offered animal sacrifices to God from the clean animals he had taken onto the ark. *"And the Lord smelled the smoothing aroma; and the Lord said to Himself, 'I will never again curse the ground on account of man, for the intent of man's heart is evil from his youth; and I will never again destroy every living thing, as I have done...'" (Genesis 8:21).* In this case, God approved of Noah's sacrifice. God does give man dominion over the animal kingdom, the right to use animals as a food source, and right of life and death. The only problem is ... with every right there is responsibility! Man must exercise with great caution those rights given to him by God. In the case of euthanasia, every animal is a divine instrument of God and man should exercise his right of life and death over that animal with great care.

When is it right to euthanize a pet? I am not sure that there is a correct answer to this question. There are times when it is easier to make a decision: when a pet is in severe pain that cannot be managed, when a pet has a terminal disease, when an animal has been injured, especially large animals, and treatment is not reasonable, or when disease has removed any hope of recovery. Cost can be a factor. When a family can no longer afford medical treatment, euthanasia is an option. I say that cost can be factor in making the decision with some trepidation. I have known families that love and provide for their pets with great care and attention but who cannot afford lengthy medical care. Cost is a part of the decision making process.

Euthanasia should be a matter of prayer. Ask God for guidance. You should discuss the matter with your pet. Not that your pet understands words or sentences, but pets do pick up on moods and emotions. Also, verbalizing helps you to clarify your options. Verify your conclusions with your veterinarian. Your veterinarian will not make the decision for you, he or she can only guide you through the decision making process.

Once a decision has been made, several other decisions are in order. Where should the euthanasia take place? Asking your veterinarian to come to you home is not out of order. Your home is a familiar and non-threat-

❖ ❖ ❖ *Animals* ❖ ❖ ❖

ening place for you and your pet; possibly your pet's favorite place. Always, a veterinary clinic is available.

Euthanasia should be quick and painless. Your veterinarian will probably ask you to sign a legal release, authorizing him or her to perform the euthanasia. Some veterinarians tranquilize an animal prior to injecting the euthanizing solution. Under the tranquilizer, the animal becomes drowsy or sleepy and remains very calm during the entire process. Resistance by the pet is to a needle prick or to being restrained. Normally a euthanizing solution is injected into a vein and death occurs immediately, in a matter of seconds. The injected solution is given in a concentration that is strong enough to impair normal body functions. Breathing ceases, the heart stops, and death occurs when all vital signs cease to exist. The entire process is over in seconds. Involuntary muscle movements or twitching can, and occasionally will, occur but that should not stress a pet owner, it is natural and does not mean that the animal is still alive.

The pet owner and possibly the entire family, if

🐾 🐾 🐾 Dr. Joe King 🐾 🐾 🐾

appropriate, should be present during euthanasia. The owners' presence has a calming effect on the pet and there should be some closure when the pet owner sees that all pain and suffering has ceased.

Sometimes it is difficult to say anything after a pet has been euthanized. Silence is okay. If something needs to be said, let me offer a prayer:

> *From out of the ground, Thou has formed all*
> *living things,*
> *Thou dost send forth Thy Spirit,*
> *They are created;*
> *The earth is full of Thy possessions*
> *Thou dost take away their spirit,*
> *they expire.*
> *(Name of Pet) has served Thee well.*
> *Amen.*

Veterinarians should allow the owner to spend time alone with the pet after euthanasia. Time alone gives

❖ ❖ ❖ *Animals* ❖ ❖ ❖

the owner an opportunity to say good-bye. Veterinarians understand the significance of the loss of a pet and can offer some guidance on grief or point you in the right direction for counseling. Help is also available through your minister and even on the Internet.

A veterinarian may ask a pet owner for permission to perform a necropsy, an animal autopsy. Many valuable lessons can be learned from a necropsy and a pet owner should consider the possible benefits.

Some veterinarians will provide for disposing of the remains. In many cases it is wise to take the remains home and hold a funeral or memorial service. A funeral service can provide closure and is an opportunity to provide one final loving act for the pet. Also, in the case of children, a funeral service can be a valuable tool in teaching the values of life and something about the mortality of man and all living things.

🐾 🐾 🐾 Dr. Joe King 🐾 🐾 🐾

Love

❖ ❖ ❖ *Animals* ❖ ❖ ❖

Raphael
The Vision of Ezekiel (1518)
Pitti Gallery, Florence

Funeral Services for Pets

As a ministerial student, I was taught that the funeral service was an important part of the grieving process. Almost every culture has developed ceremonies and practices to honor the dead and comfort those left behind.

A funeral service is more. Death has a way of crippling our desire to function and the funeral service requires planning and preparation. In many cultures, the funeral service occurs immediately after death, but in the United States the service is postponed and any delay requires embalming to preserve the body. When a beloved pet dies, the funeral service should be performed as soon as possible and, if practical, the same day the death occurs.

A funeral service serves as a memorial and is a way to honor life and glorify the Creator of all life.

❀ ❀ ❀ *Animals* ❀ ❀ ❀

Services may include hymns, poems, other music and eulogies.

Typically, a funeral service follows the traditional pattern of a song, opening prayer, reading of the obituary, song, Old Testament reading, New Testament reading, sermon or eulogies and, finally, a closing prayer.

There are no rules in planning a funeral service and you should not feel obligated to follow any certain pattern. The most important aspect of any funeral service is that it ministers to the needs of family and friends of those who have lost something very near and dear.

The best place to hold a service would be at the grave of a pet. You should determine ahead of time what to use as a casket; a cardboard box or some other type of container. The making of a grave marker or headstone can be a kind and healing act. A simple cross made of sticks or a more elaborate stone marker are possibilities. The family should gather around the graveside, probably best after the pet has been buried, and then join together

❈ ❈ ❈ Dr. Joe King ❈ ❈ ❈

in a memorial service, if possible, with all playing a part.

May I suggest the following as an examples of short and simple services than can be modified or rearranged to met your needs. The following are only examples to help you get started:

EXAMPLE 1

I. Opening Prayer

Dear Heavenly Father,
Thank you for sending (name of pet)
into our lives,
Please be close to us in our loss,
Help us to understand that life is sacred,
In our pain, bring to us peace,
In our loss, comfort us with your presence.
Amen.

II. Read Psalms 104

24 O Lord how many are Thy Works
In wisdom Thou hast made them all
The earth is full of Thy possessions.

25 There is the sea, great and broad

❖ ❖ ❖ *Animals* ❖ ❖ ❖

In which are swarms without number
Animals both small and great

27 They all wait for Thee
To give them their food in due season.

28 Thou dost give to them , they gather it up;
Thou dost open Thy hand, they are satisfied with good,

29 Thou dost hide Thy face, they are dismayed;
Thou dost take away their spirit, they expire,
And return to their dust.

30 Thou dost send forth Thy Spirit, they are created;
And Thou dost renew the face of the ground.

III. Read a prepared statement honoring your pet. It would be a good idea to let each member of the family contribute some part.

IV. Closing prayer.

Our Heavenly Father,
Thank you for life and for sharing
(Name of Pet) with us
Give us wisdom to understand the sacredness of life,
And give us strength to face death
knowing that death is not an end,
but the beginning.
Amen.

🐾 🐾 🐾 Dr. Joe King 🐾 🐾 🐾

EXAMPLE 2

I. Read an obituary of your pet. The obituary could be a brief history of how he/she came into your life, how he/she changed your life, or highlights of your experiences together.

II. Read from Isaiah 11

> 6 *And the wolf will dwell with the lamb,*
> *and the leopard will lie down with the kid,*
> *And the calf and the young lion*
> *and the fatling together;*
> *And the little boy will lead them.*
>
> 7 *And the cow and the bear will graze*
> *Their young will lie down together;*
> *And the lion will eat straw like the ox.*
>
> 8 *And the nursing child will play*
> *by the hole of the cobra*
> *And the weaned child will put his hand*
> *on the viper's den.*
>
> 9 *They will not hurt or destroy*
> *in all My holy mountain*
> *For the earth will be full*
> *of the knowledge of the Lord*
> *As the waters cover the sea.*

❖ ❖ ❖ *Animals* ❖ ❖ ❖

III. Closing. Close with a poem, the 23rd Psalm, or prayer.

Psalms 23

*1 The Lord is my shepherd,
I shall not want.*

*2 He make me lie down in green pastures;
He leads me beside quiet waters.*

*3 He restore my soul;
He guides me in the paths of righteousness
For His name's sake*

*4 Even though I walk through the valley
of the shadow of death,
I fear no evil; for Thou are with me;
Thy rod and Thy staff, they comfort me.*

*5 Thou dost prepare a table before me
in the presence of my enemies;
Thou hast anointed my head with oil;
My cup overflows,*

*6 Surely goodness and loving kindness
will follow me all the days of my life,
And I will dwell in the house of the Lord forever.*

❂ ❂ ❂ Dr. Joe King ❂ ❂ ❂

Example # 3

I. Open with a prayer:

*Creator of heaven and earth,
we thank You for life great and small.
Not one sparrow falls to the ground
that You are not aware of.
Not only did You create all living things,
You gather them unto Yourself for eternity.
Today we are here to thank You
for bringing (name of pet) into our lives.
Teach us the value of life
and comfort us in death.
Amen.*

II. Read Genesis 1:24.25

24 *Then God said, "Let the earth bring forth living
creatures after their kind;
cattle and creeping things and the beasts
of the earth after their kind";
and it was so.*

25 *And God made the beasts of the earth
after their kind;
and the cattle after their kind;*

*and everything that creeps on the ground
after its kind;
and God saw that it was good.*

III. Read a poem or a short written history of your pet.

IV. Close by reading Revelation 21:4

*"He shall wipe away every tear from their eyes;
and there shall no longer be any death;
There shall no longer be any mourning
or crying or pain;
the first things have passed away."*

You should not feel obligated to use the above examples. Mix or match the examples to meet your specific need. Use other passages. The appendix of this book contains many other references to animals throughout the bible. Pick those passages that meet your needs, use poems, funny stories about your pet, or just speak from

🐾 🐾 🐾 Dr. Joe King 🐾 🐾 🐾

the heart. Remember, there is no wrong way to eulogize your pet if the service meets your needs. Most of all remember, God understands your grief.

🐾 🐾 🐾 *Animals* 🐾 🐾 🐾

Giotto (1266? - 1337)
The Entry into Jerusalem
Arena Chapel, Padua

🐾 🐾 🐾 Dr. Joe King 🐾 🐾 🐾

APPENDIX A
Prayers for Animals

Hear our humble prayer,
O God,
for our friends the animals, your creatures.
We Pray especially for all that are suffering in any way:
for the overworked and underfed,
the hunted, lost, or hungry;
for all in captivity or ill-treated,
and for those that must be put to death.
For those who deal with them
we ask a heart of compassion,
gentle hands,
and
kindly words.
Make us all true friends to animals
and so to share
the blessings
of the merciful.
Amen

Albert Schweitzer

🐾 🐾 🐾 *Animals* 🐾 🐾 🐾

O Heavenly Father,
Creator of all living things.

We ask your blessings
upon the animals that surround us.

Give to us compassion and understanding
and give our animal friends
peace and comfort.

Bless these animals that
give us companionship.
Through them, teach us
the value of life
and the joy of service.

Joe King

I will extol Thee,
My God, O King;
And I will bless Thy name
forever and ever.

Thou dost open Thy hand,
And dost satisfy the desire of
every living thing.

Psalms 145:1,16

🐾 🐾 🐾   Dr. Joe King   🐾 🐾 🐾

O Heavenly Father,
protect and bless all things that have breath.
Guard them from all evil,
and let them sleep in peace.*

O God,
You created al living things
on the face of the earth
and gave us dominion over them:
Grant that we may be faithful to this trust
in the way we treat all animals,
both wild and tame.
Teach us to admire their beauty
and
to delight in their cunning; to
respect their strength
and
to wonder at their intelligence.
Grant that our use of them maybe both merciful and
wise.
so we may lend our voice to their praise of your
goodness
which, endures forever. *
Amen

Almighty God,
who has given us richly all things to enjoy;
bless, we beseech you, these animals
which we offer in your name and presence;
that, caring for them with grateful hearts,
we may know even more the joy of your creation,
through Jesus Christ our Lord.
Amen*

*From Saint Francis on the Hill, Episcopal Church
El Paso, Texas
The Blessing of Animals

Animals

Praise the Lord from the earth,
Sea monsters and all deeps;
Fire and hail, snow and clouds;
Stormy wind, fulfilling His word;
Mountains and all hills;
Fruit trees and all cedars;
Beasts and all cattle;
Creeping things, and winged fowl;
Kings of the earth and all peoples;
Princes and all judges of the earth;
Both young men and virgins;
Old men and children.
Let them praise the name of the Lord
For His name alone is exalted;
His glory is above earth and heaven.

Psalms 148-7-13

Let everything that has breath praise the Lord.
Praise the Lord

Psalms 150:6

❖ ❖ ❖ Dr. Joe King ❖ ❖ ❖

A PRAYER FOR A LOST PET

Our Dearest Heavenly Father,
Creator and Sustainer of all living things;
We lift to you our lost and missing pet.
Please give our lost companion a guiding light,
a guardian angel,
to help bring him/her safely home.
Protect him/her from the dangers
that lurk along the roadside,
and lead him/her to those
with friendly and compassionate
hearts.
Amen

A PRAYER FOR A SICK ANIMAL

O Heavenly Father,
Creator of Life,
Sustainer,
We lift to you our sick pet.
Give to those who care for
him/her wisdom and knowledge.
Wisdom to know the causes of illness
and the knowledge to administer
an effective and appropriate
treatment.
Amen

APPENDIX B
Bible References to Animals

Bible References to Animals in the Old Testament
Note: The following is only a partial listing of animal references

Genesis

1:20-23	God creates sea life, birds, sea monster
1:24-25	God creates cattle, creeping things, beast of the field
1:26-28	God creates Man in His own image and gives him dominion over all living things
1:29-30	God gives plants and fruit as a food source to man and animal
2:18-20	Detailed account of the creation of animal life, Animals are formed from the ground Animals are created as companions to man Man names all living creatures
3:1-7	Fall of man
3:21	The Lord makes garments of skin for Adam and his wife and clothed them
5:1	God makes Adam in the likness of God
6:7	God is sorry that He made man and animals
6:1-13	The causes of the Genesis Flood
6:14-8:19	The Genesis Flood
6:18-20	God establishes a covenant with Noah, Noah's family and the animal kingdom
6:21	God commands Noah to take food for

♣ ♣ ♣ Dr. Joe King ♣ ♣ ♣

	himself and the animals onto the ark
7:1-3, 8	Clean animals are taken into the ark by sevens, unclean animals by two's, male and female
7:14-16	Noah takes representatives of all living things into the ark
7:21-23	All living things not on the ark perish in the flood
8:20-21	Noah offers an animals sacrifice to God God accepts the sacrifice and promises never again to destroy every living thing
9:2	God places the fear of man upon the animal kingdom
9:3	God gives to man animals as a food source, as he had given the plants
9:8-11	God's covenant with man and the animal kingdom
9:12-17	God gives the rainbow as a sign of His covenant
30:32-43	Jacob's exercise in animal reproduction

Leviticus

11:1-47	The laws concerning food,
16:5-28	Offerings for the day of Atonement
17:1-16	Laws concerning sacrifices
25:1-7	The Sabbatical year, benefits the animals
11:1-35	God provides quail to the people of Israel
22:21-41	Balaam's donkey The donkey sees the Angel of The Lord The donkey speaks Balaam is chastised by the Angel of The Lord for beating his donkey

Kings

17:2-24	The ravens provide for Elijah near the

❧ ❧ ❧ *Animals* ❧ ❧ ❧

Job

34:14-15	Elihu's speech concerning the Spirit of God

Psalms

8:4-9	The Psalmist declares that man has dominion over all things
36:6	The Lord preserves man and beast
50:10-11	Every beast belongs to God, He knows every bird of the mountain
84:3	The bird and the swallow have found a home in the house of God
104:29-30	God takes away their breath, they die He sends forth his spirit and they are created

Ecclesiastes

3:19-21	Fate of the sons of men and of beast is the same, all go to the same place

Isaiah

11:6-9	The peaceable kingdom, the wolf will dwell with the lamb and the lion will eat straw like the ox

Ezekiel

1:4-14	Ezekiel's vision of the four living creatures with the face of a man, lion, bull and eagle

Jonah

1:15	Jonah is thrown overboard
1:17	The Lord appoints a great fish to swallow Jonah

🐾 🐾 🐾 Dr. Joe King 🐾 🐾 🐾

2:10   The Lord commands the fish to spit Jonah onto dry land

Bible References in the New Testament

Matthew

3:16   The Spirit of God descends upon Jesus as a dove after His baptism
6:26   Your heavenly Father feeds and cares for the birds of the air, are you not worth more than they?
8:28-34   Jesus cast demons from two men into a herd of swine
The swine rush into the sea and perish
12:11-12   Jesus' sermon on the lost sheep and the Sabbath
21:1-11   Jesus enters Jerusalem on the back of a donkey colt
26:74   A cock announces Peter's betrayal of Jesus

Mark

1:11   Mark reports the Spirit of God descending upon Jesus like a dove after his baptism
1:13   After His Temptation, Jesus is in the wilderness with the wild beast.
The Angels minister to Him
5:1-20   Jesus cast demons into a herd of swine
The swine are drowned in the sea
6:38-44   Jesus feeds the multitude with five loaves and two fish
11:1-11   The Triumphal Entry into Jerusalem
Jesus enters Jerusalem on a colt, on which no one yet has ever sat.
14:72   A cock announces the betrayal of Jesus

❖ ❖ ❖ *Animals* ❖ ❖ ❖

by Peter

Luke

2:7	Jesus is born in a manger
3:22	After being baptized, the Spirit of God descends upon Jesus in the bodily form of a dove
5:4-7	Jesus tells Simon Peter where to catch fish
8:26-39	Jesus cast demons into a herd of swine
19:28-44	Jesus enters Jerusalem on the back of a colt
22:60-61	A cock announces the betrayal of Jesus by Peter

John

12:12-19	The Triumphal entry

Acts

10:9-19	Peter's vision of food animals and God's announcement that everything is clean

Corinthians

9:9	Paul writes about Deuteronomy 25:4, you shall not muzzle the ox while threshing referencing the value of a laborer
15:39	Not all flesh is the same

Hebrews

9:11-13	The Blood of Christ, not the blood of animal sacrifices cleanses your conscience

James

3:3	Bits into the horses mouth so they may

❖ ❖ ❖ Dr. Joe King ❖ ❖ ❖

	obey us
3:7	Every species of beast and birds and reptiles and creatures of seas is tamed by the human race
Revelation	
4:6-11	Four living creatures, one like a lion, one like a calf, one like man and one like an eagle
5:13	Every living thing praises God
6:1-17	The seal judgements, a white horse (2), a red horse (4), a black horse (5), a ashen horse (8)
8:9	A third of the creatures in the sea are destroyed
8:13	An eagle flying in midheaven announces woes
9:3	Locust upon the earth
13:2	A beast comes up out of the sea. He is like a lepard, bear and a lion
14:1	The Lamb on Mount Zion
16:3	The bowl judgement Every living thing in the sea
19:11	Christ on a white horse
19:14	Armies of Christ in heaven on white horses
19:17	Birds which fly in midheaven are told to "assemble for the great supper of God."
21:4	No longer death, mourning, crying or
22:3	In the New Jerusalem, no longer any curse

❖ ❖ ❖ *Animals* ❖ ❖ ❖

Love
ANIMALS